TRUST ISSUES

A Beginner's Guide to Protecting Your New Fortune

Michael Markuson

Nerdpicker Press

Disclaimer

The information provided in this eBook, *"Trust Issues: A Beginner's Guide to Protecting Your New Fortune,"* is for educational and informational purposes only. It is **not** intended to serve as financial, legal, or professional advice. While we aim to provide helpful tips and general knowledge about trusts, we are **not** lawyers, financial advisors, or tax professionals.

Before making any decisions regarding your financial future, setting up a trust, or managing a windfall, you should **always** consult with a qualified attorney, licensed financial advisor, or tax professional.

The laws and regulations surrounding trusts and wealth management vary by location and individual circumstances, so it's important to get advice tailored specifically to your situation.

This eBook is not a substitute for professional guidance, and no legal, financial, or tax-related outcomes are guaranteed based on the content here. The authors assume no responsibility for any decisions or actions taken based on the information provided.

In short: **Don't just trust us—trust the professionals!**

"Still it is good info and I recommend it!"
- *Mike*

TABLE OF CONTENTS

Chapter 1: What the Heck is a Trust?
Chapter 2: Sudden Wealth Syndrome: Trust Issues (and Why You Need One)
Chapter 3: Revocable vs. Irrevocable Trusts: The Great Debat
Chapter 4: Trust Me, Your Family Will Thank You
Chapter 5: Taxes, Schmaxes: How Trusts Save You Money
Chapter 6: Who's the Boss? Choosing Your Trustee Wisely
Chapter 7: Living the Dream: How to Use a Living Trust
Chapter 8: Trust Funds Aren't Just for the Super Rich
Chapter 9: Protecting Your Assets from Everyone, Including Yourself
Chapter 10: The Final Step: How to Set Up a Trust

MIKE MARKUSON

CHAPTER 1: WHAT THE HECK IS A TRUST?

Summary:

In this chapter, we'll break down what a trust actually is—without the legal mumbo-jumbo. Think of it like a box where you stash your money, property, or other goodies, and someone (called a trustee) manages it for you or your heirs. We'll keep things simple, explaining the basic structure and why it might be the smartest move after you hit it big.

So, you've hit it big—whether it's through a lottery win, a once-in- a-lifetime inheritance, or, as some of your friends might hope, the revaluation of foreign currency like Iraqi Dinar or Vietnamese Dong. Suddenly, you've got more money than you ever imagined, and it's both exciting and a little scary. What now? You keep hearing about trusts, but what the heck are they? Let's dive into it, and don't worry

we're keeping this simple. **What**

is a Trust, Really?

Imagine you have a treasure chest (stay with me here). In that chest, you stash your valuables: money, property, or anything else that's important to you. But instead of guarding that chest yourself, you hire someone (called a *trustee*) to watch over it for you. You tell them who can take treasure out, when they can do it, and how much they can have. That's essentially what a trust is—only instead of gold doubloons, we're talking cold, hard cash, real estate, and other assets.

A trust is a **legal arrangement** where one party (the trustee) holds and manages assets for another party (the beneficiaries). You, the person setting up the trust, are called the **grantor** (or trustor, settlor —fancy terms that all mean the same thing). You put your assets in the trust, tell the trustee how to manage them, and decide who benefits from it.

Here's why it's smart: a trust helps you control your wealth even when you're not around. Whether it's to avoid taxes, keep your family from fighting over your stuff, or make sure your newfound riches don't disappear faster than you can say "revaluation," a trust has your back.

The Main Players in a Trust

Let's break this down so it's clear who's involved in this whole trust business:

- **Grantor (that's you):** The person who creates the trust and puts assets into it.
- **Trustee (the responsible one):** The person or company you choose to manage the trust. Think of them as the manager of your treasure chest. They follow your instructions and look out for the best interests of the people you want to benefit from the trust.
- **Beneficiaries (the lucky ones):** These are the people (or organizations) who get to enjoy the goodies from the trust. That could be your family, friends, or even a charity.

Why You Might Need a Trust

You might be thinking, "Okay, but I'm not a billionaire. Do I really need a trust?" Well, the answer is: **probably!** Especially if you've suddenly come into a significant amount of wealth and want to protect it for the future. Here's why:

- **Avoid Probate:** Probate is the legal process that happens after someone dies, and trust me, it's a pain in the neck. It's slow, it's expensive, and it's public. A trust helps you avoid all that drama, keeping your assets safe and passing them on
to your heirs without a drawn-out legal process.

- **Keep Control:** You can set up rules about how your money is handled, even if you're no longer around to call the shots. Want your kids to get their inheritance only after they turn 30? Done. Want to make sure a chunk of your wealth goes to charity? Easy. You're in charge.

- **Protect Your Wealth:** Without a trust, your money could be at risk from lawsuits, creditors, or even a messy divorce. A trust can help shield your assets and keep them safe from people who might come knocking at your door with a hand out.

Trust vs. Will: What's the Difference?

You've probably heard of wills, too, and you might be wondering how a trust is different. Here's a quick and easy way to think about it:

- **A Will** tells people what to do with your stuff after you're gone, but it has to go through probate court, which, as we mentioned, is a hassle.
- **A Trust** lets you decide how your stuff is managed while you're alive *and* after you're gone. No probate, no court, just a smooth handoff of your assets according to your rules.

Think of a will as a one-time instruction manual for after you're gone, while a trust is like a remote control—you can use it during your life and beyond.

Types of Trusts (More on These Later)

There are different types of trusts for different situations, and we'll dive into those later in the book. But just to give you a sneak peek:

- **Revocable Trusts:** You can change them anytime while you're alive (you're still in control).
- **Irrevocable Trusts:** Once they're set up, you can't change them (but they have some pretty sweet tax benefits).

Don't worry—we'll cover all the details in future chapters, so you'll know exactly which type might be right for you.

The Bottom Line

A trust is a smart way to protect your newfound wealth, manage it according to your wishes, and keep things running smoothly even when you're not there. It's like hiring a super-organized manager for your fortune, so you can kick back and enjoy your success without worrying about what happens next.

Now that you've got a basic understanding of what a trust is, we'll dive deeper into why you might want one, the different types available, and how to set one up. Stick around—it's not as complicated (or as boring) as it sounds!

TRUST ISSUES: A BEGINNER'S GUIDE TO PROTECTING YOUR NEW FORTUNE

CHAPTER 2: SUDDEN WEALTH SYNDROME: TRUST ISSUES (AND WHY YOU NEED ONE)

Summary:

When your bank account goes from zero to hero overnight, your life can get complicated fast. We'll talk about what happens when you suddenly become wealthy and why creating a trust can help you manage that pile of cash responsibly, protect your wealth from greedy hands, and avoid common "new money" mistakes.

Congratulations! You've won the lottery, cashed in on a huge investment, or—if the rumors are true—your foreign currency just revalued, and you're suddenly rolling in money. It's like a dream come true, right? Well, sort of. With great wealth comes great responsibility, and that's where things can get tricky. Ever heard of **Sudden Wealth Syndrome**? Yep, it's a thing. And trust me, it's something you want to avoid.

In this chapter, we'll talk about what happens when your bank account skyrockets overnight, why it can mess with your life (and your brain), and how a trust can help you manage this windfall before it manages you.

What Is Sudden Wealth Syndrome?

Sudden Wealth Syndrome (SWS) is what happens when people who aren't used to having lots of money suddenly find themselves with a fortune. Think of lottery winners, professional athletes, or your buddy who invested in the right stock at the right time. It sounds great on the surface, but it can lead to all sorts of problems—financial, emotional, and even social.

Here's what can happen:
- **Overspending:** It's easy to think the money will never run out, but trust me, it can (and fast!). Without a plan, you might splurge on fancy cars, new houses, and endless vacations until one day you look at your bank account and wonder where it all went.

- **Family and Friends:** Everyone's your best friend when you've got money, right? Suddenly, long-lost cousins, childhood pals, and even people you barely know start showing up asking for "loans" (which, by the way, you'll probably never see again). This can lead to awkward situations, strained relationships, and lots of guilt.

- **Bad Investments:** You're now the person with "the money," and everyone has a *great* business idea they want you to fund. The problem? Most of these ventures are as risky as betting on a three-legged horse. One wrong move, and you could lose a big chunk of your wealth.

- **Stress and Anxiety:** Believe it or not, having too much money can stress you out. Decisions about how to manage it, keep it safe, and handle the sudden change in lifestyle can cause major anxiety. You might even feel disconnected from the life you had before.

In short, sudden wealth can feel overwhelming. It's like getting a new toy, but with no instruction manual—and no one wants to break their shiny new toy.

Trust Issues: Why a Trust is Your New Best Friend

So how do you avoid Sudden Wealth Syndrome and keep your money—and your sanity? Enter the **trust**. Setting up a trust isn't just for rich old people or billionaires. It's for anyone who wants to protect their money, make smart decisions, and avoid all the pitfalls that come with a sudden financial windfall.

Here's why a trust can save you from all that drama:

1. **You Stay in Control**
    Even though you've got a trustee (someone you've appointed to manage the trust), you still get to call the shots. Want to give your cousin a loan? Go ahead. But if you don't trust yourself to say "no" when someone asks for money, a trust can set limits. You can put rules in place to control how much money you (or others) can access and when.

2. **Avoid Family Feuds**
    Money can tear families apart faster than a Thanksgiving dinner gone wrong. A trust lets you lay down the law, deciding who gets what and when. If you've got specific plans for your money (like leaving a chunk to charity or making sure your kids don't blow their inheritance on video games and designer sneakers), the trust enforces those wishes. No one gets to argue—your trust is legally binding.

3. **Keep Your Money Safe**
   The more money you have, the more likely someone will try to take it—whether it's through lawsuits, divorces, or greedy creditors. A trust can act like a financial fortress, protecting your assets from all those who might want a piece of the pie. It's harder for people to go after your money if it's tucked away in a well-structured trust.

4. **Say Goodbye to Impulsive Spending**
   We get it—you're suddenly rich, and it's tempting to blow money on whatever catches your eye. But a trust can help rein in that spending. You can set rules about how much you're allowed to take out each year or require trustee approval for major purchases. It's like having an extra layer of protection between you and those impulse buys.

But Do I Really Need One Right Now?

You might have heard some folks say, "You don't need a trust now, just wait until after the revaluation (RV) or the big payout." But the truth is, **the earlier you start thinking about a trust, the better**. Here's why:

- **Planning Ahead**: Sudden wealth doesn't come with a warning label. You need to be prepared. By setting up a trust now, you've already got a plan in place for when the money lands in your lap. You can make thoughtful decisions without the pressure of a ticking clock or a flood of people wanting a piece of your newfound wealth.

- **Protecting Assets**: Even before your wealth shows up, putting a trust in place can help you avoid issues down the line. For example, if you expect a big RV or currency revaluation, having a trust ready ensures that your money is immediately protected, and you don't have to scramble after the fact.

- **Peace of Mind**: There's a lot to be said for knowing you've got a solid plan. Having a trust gives you peace of mind, knowing that no matter what happens with your money, you're prepared. Plus, you won't have to worry about someone taking advantage of your new wealth.

Types of Trusts for Sudden Wealth (A Preview)

While we'll dive deeper into the different kinds of trusts later, here's a quick look at the two main options you'll want to think about if you're facing sudden wealth:

- **Revocable Trust:** This is the flexible one. You can change the terms whenever you want, and you still have full control over the assets. It's a great starting point because it lets you adapt as your financial situation evolves.
- **Irrevocable Trust:** This one's more permanent. Once it's set up, you can't make changes easily. But the benefit

is that it offers stronger protection from taxes, creditors, and lawsuits. It's like locking your fortune in a vault that even you can't open without jumping through hoops.

The Bottom Line

Sudden wealth is a life-changing experience, but it can also bring a host of challenges—financial, emotional, and social. By creating a trust, you can take control of your new fortune and protect it from the things (and people) that might try to take it away from you. A trust isn't just a tool for the ultra-rich; it's a smart move for anyone looking to secure their financial future.

And remember: having money doesn't mean you have to handle everything alone. A trust lets you delegate some of the responsibility, helping you make the most of your windfall while avoiding the headaches that come with it.

Next up, we'll dive into the two main types of trusts: revocable and irrevocable. Which one is right for you? Let's find out in Chapter 3!

MIKE MARKUSON

CHAPTER 3: REVOCABLE VS. IRREVOCABLE TRUSTS: THE GREAT DEBATE

Summary:

Time to get into the nitty-gritty of the two main types of trusts. In this chapter, we'll explain what makes a revocable trust flexible (you can change it anytime) and why an irrevocable trust is more rigid (you can't mess with it once it's set up). We'll also look at when each type makes sense and what you should consider as you plan for your new fortune.

Alright, so you've come to terms with the fact that you need a trust. Good choice! But now you're faced with the big question: **Should you go with a revocable trust or an irrevocable trust?** It might sound like a "pick your poison" situation, but it's actually not that bad. Both types of trusts can help you protect your fortune, but they do it in very different ways. Let's break down the pros, cons, and key differences so you can figure out which one is right for you.

What's the Difference, Anyway?

Think of a **revocable trust** like a flexible gym membership—

you can change it whenever you want. You're still in control, and if your life situation changes, you can adjust the terms of the trust. If you want to take assets out, put more in, or even dissolve the trust altogether, you can. This makes it a great option for people who like to stay in the driver's seat.

An **irrevocable trust**, on the other hand, is like signing a contract with no opt-out clause. Once it's set up, you can't change it (well, you *technically* can, but it's complicated and expensive). Why would anyone want to do that, you ask? Because irrevocable trusts offer some serious perks when it comes to protecting your wealth from taxes, creditors, and lawsuits.

Now, let's dig into the details.

THE CASE FOR REVOCABLE TRUSTS

A **revocable trust** is, as the name suggests, revocable—meaning you can change it, tweak it, or even cancel it altogether if you decide it's not working for you. Here's why you might want to consider one:

1. You Stay in Control

With a revocable trust, you're the boss. You can still access and use your assets as if nothing has changed. Want to sell a property you put in the trust? Go for it. Need to pull some money out for that once-in-a-lifetime vacation? No problem. You can make adjustments, add new assets, and change the beneficiaries as your situation evolves.

2. Avoid Probate

One of the biggest reasons people set up revocable trusts is to avoid probate court when they pass away. Probate is the legal process where a court validates your will and distributes your assets—and it's slow, expensive, and can lead to family drama. With a revocable trust, your assets go directly to your beneficiaries without the need for probate. Your family gets their inheritance faster, and everything stays private (no nosy neighbors finding out who got what).

3. Flexibility for Changing Circumstances

Life changes—maybe you have another kid, or your financial situation shifts. A revocable trust is flexible enough to adapt. You can change the beneficiaries, the terms of the trust, and even who's in charge (the trustee). This makes it ideal for someone who wants to keep options open.

But There's a Catch…

While revocable trusts are flexible, they don't offer much in the way of asset protection. Because you still have control over the trust, creditors and lawsuits can still come after the assets in it. If you get sued, the money in a revocable trust is fair game. And since the assets are technically still yours, they're not shielded from estate taxes after you pass away. That's where an irrevocable trust comes in.

THE CASE FOR IRREVOCABLE TRUSTS

An **irrevocable trust** is like locking your assets in a vault and giving someone else the key. Once you set it up, you give up control over the assets inside (don't panic, we'll explain why this isn't as scary as it sounds). Why would you want to do this? Because it offers stronger protections for your wealth and some pretty sweet tax benefits.

1. Asset Protection

The biggest advantage of an irrevocable trust is that it shields your assets from creditors, lawsuits, and even ex-spouses (in case things get ugly). Once your assets are in an irrevocable trust, they are no longer considered yours. This means that if someone sues you, they can't go after what's in the trust. It's like having a financial force field around your money.

2. Estate Tax Benefits

When you die, Uncle Sam will be looking for his cut of your estate. An irrevocable trust helps reduce the amount of estate taxes your heirs have to pay. Since the assets in the trust aren't considered part of your estate anymore, they're not subject to estate taxes. This can save your heirs a ton of money—and let's face it, no one wants to pay more taxes than they have to.

3. Planning for Long-Term Care

If you ever need long-term care, like staying in a nursing home, an irrevocable trust can protect your assets from being drained by medical bills. If your assets are in an irrevocable trust, they generally won't count against you when you apply for Medicaid. That means you can qualify for benefits while still protecting your wealth for your family.

The Downsides...

Giving up control isn't easy. With an irrevocable trust, you can't just decide to take your assets back or change the terms on a whim. Once it's set up, it's pretty much set in stone. Plus, irrevocable trusts are more complicated and expensive to set up than revocable ones.

You'll need to work with a good attorney to get it right. But if you're serious about protecting your wealth, an irrevocable trust might be worth the hassle.

WHICH ONE IS RIGHT FOR YOU?

Here's a simple way to think about it:

- If you want **flexibility** and to stay in control of your assets while you're alive, go with a **revocable trust**.

- If you're looking for **strong protection** against lawsuits, creditors, and estate taxes, and you're willing to give up control, an **irrevocable trust** is the way to go.

But it's not always an either/or situation. You can actually have both! Many people start with a revocable trust to keep things flexible, then set up an irrevocable trust later on when they're ready to lock things down and focus on asset protection. This way, you can enjoy the benefits of both types of trusts depending on where you are in life.

TRUSTS IN ACTION: REAL-LIFE EXAMPLES

Let's take a look at how a revocable and an irrevocable trust might play out in real life:

- **Example 1: The Revocable Trust Route**
  Meet Jessica. Jessica just won a huge lottery prize, and while she's not sure what she wants to do with all that money just yet, she knows she doesn't want it sitting unprotected. She sets up a **revocable trust**, which allows her to control her assets, avoid probate, and decide how she wants to distribute her wealth. A few years down the road, after careful planning, Jessica decides to set up an irrevocable trust to better protect her fortune for her kids.

- **Example 2: The Irrevocable Trust Solution**
  Now meet Carlos. Carlos is worried about getting sued because he's a business owner, and his personal assets could be at risk. He sets up an **irrevocable trust**, which shields his assets from any potential lawsuits or creditors. Carlos knows he won't be able to change the trust easily, but he feels more secure knowing his wealth is protected no matter what happens to his business.

THE BOTTOM LINE

Deciding between a revocable and an irrevocable trust depends on what you value more—control or protection. A **revocable trust** lets you stay in the driver's seat and keep things flexible, but it won't protect your assets from lawsuits or taxes. An **irrevocable trust**, on the other hand, locks things down and gives you strong asset protection and tax benefits, but it requires you to give up control.

No matter which one you choose, having a trust in place is one of the smartest moves you can make to protect your wealth—especially after a big windfall. In the next chapter, we'll dive into how trusts can prevent family feuds, keep your estate out of probate, and make sure your wishes are honored. Stay tuned!

CHAPTER 4: TRUST ME, YOUR FAMILY WILL THANK YOU

Summary:

This chapter is all about how trusts can help you avoid family drama when it comes to inheritance. We'll explain how a trust keeps your wealth in line with your wishes, ensures smooth transitions, and prevents squabbles over who gets what. Trusts can be a family peacemaker, even if no one realizes it!

So, you've got the wealth, and you've decided to set up a trust to protect it. Great decision! Now let's talk about another reason why trusts are so valuable: **family drama prevention.** When it comes to money, even the happiest families can turn into the cast of a bad reality show—complete with fights, misunderstandings, and maybe even a lawsuit or two. But guess what? A trust can keep that chaos from ever happening.

In this chapter, we'll explain how trusts can help keep your family harmonious, why they're better than a will for managing your estate, and how they give you total control over who gets what—and when.

THE PROBLEM WITH FAMILY AND MONEY

It's an unfortunate truth: money can bring out the worst in people. Even in close-knit families, emotions run high when an inheritance is on the line. If you're suddenly wealthy and don't set up clear plans for how your money will be managed, the result can be a messy free-for-all.

Here are some common scenarios that can cause family disputes when you don't have a trust in place:

1. **"Who Gets What?"**

   When someone passes away without a clear plan (like a trust), everyone in the family has their own idea of who deserves what. Siblings might fight over the house, the family business, or even sentimental items. Without specific instructions, these arguments can drag on for months—or even years—in court.

2. **Probate Problems**

   Without a trust, your estate goes through **probate**—a court- supervised process where a judge decides how to distribute your assets according to your will (if you have one) or state laws (if you don't). Probate is public, time-consuming, and can lead to even more family disputes, as people feel left out or cheated.

3. **Competing Heirs**

   If you've got kids from multiple marriages, estranged relatives, or friends who are like family, things can get complicated fast. Who gets what? How do you make sure everyone is treated fairly? Without clear instructions, this can lead to tension and misunderstandings.

4. **Spouses and Significant Others**

   New marriages or long-term relationships can throw another wrench into the works. Should your spouse inherit everything? Do you want to leave something for the kids from a previous marriage? If you don't clearly define this in a trust, things can get ugly between the people you care about most.

HOW A TRUST CAN PREVENT FAMILY FEUDS

A trust lets you control the chaos by laying out clear, legally binding instructions on how your assets should be handled. Here's why this is so powerful:

1. You Make the Rules (and They Have to Follow Them)

With a trust, there's no guessing who gets what. You get to make all the decisions ahead of time. Whether you want to divide your assets equally or leave specific gifts to certain family members, the trust spells it out clearly. This eliminates any potential arguments over who's entitled to what. Your wishes are final—and legally binding.

2. No Probate Drama

One of the biggest benefits of having a trust is that it allows your family to **avoid probate** altogether. Probate can be a long, drawn-out process that leaves your loved ones waiting months (or even years) to receive their inheritance. Plus, it's public, which means anyone can see how your assets are divided. A trust bypasses all of that, so your assets go directly to the beneficiaries you've chosen, without court involvement.

3. You Control When They Get the Money

Let's say you've got kids or grandkids who aren't exactly responsible with money yet. A trust lets you control **when** they receive their inheritance. Instead of handing over a lump sum, you can stagger the payouts over time (for example, they get a portion at age 25, 30, and 35). This way, they're less likely to blow through the money in one go.

You can also set specific conditions for the distribution of assets. For instance, maybe you want your kids to only get their inheritance after they finish college or if they stay out of trouble. A trust gives you the power to do that.

4. Protecting Beneficiaries from Themselves

Sometimes, the person you're leaving money to isn't great at handling it. Maybe they're young, impulsive, or have a history of making bad decisions. A trust can set up safeguards to protect the beneficiary from their own poor judgment. For example, you can appoint a trustee to manage the assets on their behalf, ensuring they don't blow through their inheritance.

Trusts vs. Wills: Why a Trust Is the Better Choice

At this point, you might be wondering, "Can't I just leave everything in a will?" Sure, you can, but here's why a trust is usually a much better option for keeping family harmony intact:

1. Wills Go Through Probate, Trusts Don't

As we mentioned earlier, a will has to go through probate. That means your family's private matters will be dragged into court, and they'll have to wait for the probate process to finish before receiving their inheritance. Probate can also be expensive, with court fees, lawyer fees, and executor fees eating into your estate. A trust, on the other hand, avoids probate completely. The assets are distributed immediately, privately, and without the extra cost and hassle.

2. Wills Don't Offer Asset Protection

A will simply says who gets what, but it doesn't protect those assets. For example, if you leave money to a child who's in debt, creditors could come after their inheritance. With a trust, you can put protections in place to shield the assets from creditors or legal claims, making sure the money stays where it's supposed to.

3. Trusts Give You Control After You're Gone

Wills are one-and-done. Once the will is executed, that's it—the beneficiaries get their inheritance, and it's over. A trust, on the other hand, lets you keep control beyond the grave. You can stagger payouts, require certain conditions to be met, and manage the money over time to make sure it's used responsibly.

CHOOSING THE RIGHT TRUSTEE TO KEEP THE PEACE

When it comes to keeping family harmony, one of the most important decisions you'll make is choosing the **trustee**—the person who will manage the trust and make sure your instructions are followed. This is not a decision to take lightly. Picking the wrong trustee can cause just as much drama as not having a trust at all!

Here's what to consider when choosing your trustee:

- **Trustworthiness**: This one's obvious. You want someone responsible and reliable. If you're thinking about appointing a family member, ask yourself: Is this person capable of putting the needs of the beneficiaries above their own interests?
- **Fairness**: Your trustee should be impartial and fair, especially if they're managing the assets for multiple beneficiaries. You don't want someone who's going to play favorites or make biased decisions.
- **Knowledge**: Your trustee doesn't need to be a financial genius, but they should at least have some understanding of how to manage money. You can always hire a professional trustee (like a bank or trust company) if you don't have someone in your family who fits the bill.
- **Willingness**: Being a trustee can be a big responsibility, so make sure the person you choose is

up for the job. They'll need to keep detailed records, make decisions about distributions, and potentially deal with some family drama.

THE BOTTOM LINE

Family and money don't always mix well, especially when you've come into sudden wealth. Without a clear plan, even the closest families can be torn apart by inheritance disputes and misunderstandings. A trust helps you avoid all that by giving you full control over how your assets are distributed and ensuring your wishes are carried out exactly as you want.

By setting up a trust, you can keep your estate out of probate, protect your assets from creditors and lawsuits, and manage your wealth long after you're gone. Plus, your family will thank you for making things easier—and for keeping the peace when you're no longer there to mediate.

In the next chapter, we'll dive into a topic everyone hates: taxes. Don't worry—we'll make it painless. You'll learn how trusts can help you save big on taxes and protect your fortune for the long term. Stay tuned!

TRUST ISSUES: A BEGINNER'S GUIDE TO PROTECTING YOUR NEW FORTUNE

CHAPTER 5: TAXES, SCHMAXES: HOW TRUSTS SAVE YOU MONEY

Summary:

Nobody likes taxes, especially when you've just scored a windfall. We'll explain how trusts can help you legally reduce the taxes on your new wealth, preserve your money for the long haul, and make sure the IRS doesn't gobble up more than necessary. Simple, straightforward tax tips you'll actually want to read!

If there's one thing everyone can agree on, it's that taxes are a total buzzkill—especially when you've just come into a boatload of money. Suddenly, you're hearing words like "capital gains" and "estate taxes," and the government seems all too eager to grab a chunk of your newfound fortune. But don't panic! Trusts can help you keep more of your money where it belongs: in your pocket.

In this chapter, we're going to walk through how trusts can save you a fortune in taxes. Don't worry, we'll keep the jargon to a minimum and break down the basics so it's easy to understand. Trust me, you'll thank yourself later.

TRUST ISSUES: A BEGINNER'S GUIDE TO PROTECTING YOUR NEW FORTUNE

THE TAX MAN COMETH: WHAT YOU'RE UP AGAINST

Before we dive into how trusts can help, let's look at what you're trying to avoid. When you come into sudden wealth, you could be facing a variety of taxes, including:

- **Income Tax**: If your wealth comes from something like lottery winnings, you'll be hit with a hefty income tax bill. In the U.S., this can be as high as 37% depending on your total earnings.

- **Capital Gains Tax**: If you sell an asset that has appreciated in value—like stocks, real estate, or foreign currency—you'll likely owe capital gains tax on the profits. The more valuable the asset, the bigger the tax bill.

- **Estate Tax**: When you pass away, your estate (the total value of all your assets) could be subject to estate taxes. In the U.S., federal estate taxes can be as high as 40% on amounts above the exemption limit, and some states have additional estate or inheritance taxes.

- **Gift Tax**: If you want to pass some of your wealth to family members or friends while you're alive, you might have to pay gift tax on the transfer if it exceeds the annual exemption amount.

Trusts can help you minimize, or even avoid, many of these taxes. Let's take a closer look at how this works.

1. Income Tax and Trusts: Keeping the IRS at Bay

Let's say you've come into a sudden windfall—maybe through a big investment payout or the revaluation of foreign currency. In most cases, this money is treated as income, meaning it could be taxed at some of the highest rates. Luckily, trusts can help here, too.

How It Works:

If you set up an **irrevocable trust**, you can transfer your assets into the trust, and the income generated by those assets (like dividends, interest, or rental income) is taxed at the trust's rate, rather than your personal income tax rate. In some cases, this can result in significant tax savings, especially if your personal income pushes you into a higher tax bracket.

For example, if you have a stock portfolio or real estate investments, the income from those assets would normally be taxed at your personal rate. By placing them in an irrevocable trust, you shift the tax burden to the trust. And because trusts can distribute income to beneficiaries who might be in lower tax brackets (like your kids or grandkids), this spreads the wealth and reduces the overall tax hit.

Revocable Trusts and Taxes:

Keep in mind, though, that if you use a **revocable trust**, the IRS still sees the assets as yours. So, for tax purposes, it's business as usual— you'll still owe taxes on any income generated by those assets.

2. Capital Gains Tax: Cashing Out Without Getting Cleaned Out

One of the sneakiest taxes out there is **capital gains tax**—it comes into play when you sell an asset that has appreciated in value. So, if that land you bought on a whim is now worth ten times what you paid for it, or if your foreign currency revaluation turns into a jackpot, you'll likely owe capital gains tax on the profit when you cash in.

How Trusts Help:

An **irrevocable trust** can help minimize capital gains tax in two big ways:

- **Selling Through the Trust**: If you place assets into an irrevocable trust, the trust becomes the owner of those assets. When the trustee eventually sells the assets, the tax liability falls on the trust rather than on you personally. And since trusts can strategically distribute income and gains to beneficiaries, it can lower the overall tax hit.
- **Charitable Trusts**: If you're feeling philanthropic, setting up a **charitable remainder trust (CRT)** is a genius way to reduce capital gains taxes. You place highly appreciated assets (like stocks, property, or even foreign currency) into the trust, and then the trust sells the assets without triggering capital gains tax. In return, you receive an income stream from the trust, and after a set period of time, the remainder goes to charity. You get income, tax benefits, and good karma
—it's a win-win.

3. Estate Tax: Trusts vs. the Grim Reaper Tax

Estate taxes are what happen when the government decides it's not enough to tax you while you're alive—they want a piece of your pie after you die, too. If your estate exceeds a certain value (in the U.S., it's currently $12.92 million per person in 2023), you could owe up to 40% in federal estate taxes on the amount above that threshold.

Some states also have their own estate or inheritance taxes, adding to the pain.

How Trusts Help:

Trusts, especially **irrevocable trusts**, are one of the best ways to minimize estate taxes. Here's why:

- **Removing Assets from Your Estate**: When you place assets into an irrevocable trust, those assets are no longer considered part of your estate. This means they won't be subject to estate taxes when you pass away. The assets are still available to your beneficiaries (according to the terms of the trust), but they aren't included in the value of your estate for tax purposes. Goodbye, estate tax!

- **Life Insurance Trusts**: One sneaky part of estate taxes is that life insurance payouts are included in the value of your estate, even though most people don't think of life insurance as taxable. By placing your life insurance policy into an **irrevocable life insurance trust (ILIT)**, you can ensure that the death benefit goes to your beneficiaries **without** being subject to estate taxes. This is a major strategy for high-net- worth individuals looking to protect their wealth for future generations.

Estate Planning Made Simple:

Even if your estate doesn't exceed the estate tax exemption, an irrevocable trust can still help you plan for the future and avoid any surprise taxes that may come along due to changes in the law or your financial situation.

4. Gift Tax: Giving Without Losing

If you're feeling generous and want to give some of your wealth to loved ones while you're still alive, the IRS has something to say about that, too. The **gift tax** applies to any transfer of wealth over the annual exclusion limit (currently $17,000 per person in 2023). If you give more than this amount to someone in a single year, you might owe gift taxes.

How Trusts Help:

A **grantor trust**, such as a **revocable living trust**, can allow you to make gifts over time in a tax-efficient way. You can structure the trust to give smaller gifts to multiple beneficiaries each year, staying under the annual exclusion limit and avoiding gift taxes.

Another great option is an **irrevocable trust**, where you can transfer large amounts of wealth to beneficiaries all at once.

When done correctly, the gift is considered complete when the assets are placed in the trust, meaning no additional gift taxes will be owed when beneficiaries start receiving distributions.

5. The Dynasty Trust: Generational Wealth without Generational Taxes

Want to leave a lasting legacy? Enter the **dynasty trust**, an irrevocable trust designed to pass wealth down through multiple generations while skipping estate taxes along the way. It's like the ultimate cheat code for avoiding taxes while ensuring your grandkids' grandkids never have to worry about money.

How It Works:

A dynasty trust is set up to last for generations—potentially hundreds of years, depending on state laws. Once assets are placed in the trust, they can grow and compound over time without being hit with estate taxes at each generational transfer. The assets can be distributed to beneficiaries according to the terms you set, but because the trust itself doesn't die, the money stays safe from estate taxes.

This is one of the most powerful tools for creating long-term family wealth while legally sidestepping taxes.

THE BOTTOM LINE

Nobody likes paying taxes—especially when you've worked hard (or lucked out) to amass a fortune. Fortunately, trusts are one of the most effective tools for minimizing taxes and preserving your wealth. Whether you're looking to reduce income taxes, dodge capital gains taxes, or protect your estate from the taxman after you're gone, there's a trust that can help.

By setting up the right trust structure, you can pass on more of your wealth to your loved ones, make charitable contributions, and keep the IRS from getting more than its fair share. And the best part? You can do it all legally, responsibly, and with your sanity intact.

In the next chapter, we'll talk about choosing the right trustee— because, trust me, you don't want to hand over the keys to your fortune to just anyone. Stay tuned!

TRUST ISSUES: A BEGINNER'S GUIDE TO PROTECTING YOUR NEW FORTUNE

CHAPTER 6: WHO'S THE BOSS? CHOOSING YOUR TRUSTEE WISELY

Summary:

Picking the right trustee is like choosing the CEO of your personal fortune. This chapter covers what a trustee does, why you should think twice before handing the reins to Cousin Jerry, and what makes a good (or bad) trustee. We'll offer tips on how to pick someone trustworthy and competent to manage your trust.

So, you're convinced that setting up a trust is the way to go, and you're ready to protect your newfound fortune from taxes, lawsuits, and family drama. But now comes one of the most important decisions in the entire process: **choosing your trustee.** This person (or company) will be responsible for managing the trust and carrying out your wishes after you're gone. Basically, they'll hold the keys to your kingdom.

In this chapter, we're going to help you navigate the process of picking the right trustee. Spoiler alert: It's not as simple as picking your best friend or the cousin who *seems* responsible. We'll talk about what makes a good trustee, who you should avoid, and why this decision could make or break your trust plan.

WHAT DOES A TRUSTEE ACTUALLY DO?

Before we get into who should be your trustee, let's take a quick look at what a trustee actually **does.** This isn't just a title you hand out to your favorite family member—it's a serious job that comes with legal responsibilities.

Here's a breakdown of a trustee's main duties:

- **Manage the Assets**: The trustee's job is to make sure the assets in the trust are managed properly. This could involve investing money, maintaining property, or handling business interests. They have a legal duty (called a **fiduciary duty**) to manage the trust in the best interest of the beneficiaries. In other words, they can't blow the money on wild vacations or risky investments.
- **Distribute the Assets**: The trustee is also responsible for making sure the beneficiaries get their share of the trust according to your instructions. If you set up specific rules for how and when the money is distributed (like staggered payouts or conditional gifts), the trustee has to follow those rules to the letter.
- **Keep Records**: A good trustee needs to be organized. They'll have to keep detailed records of all the transactions, distributions, and tax filings related to the trust. This ensures there's a paper trail if anyone questions how the trust is being managed.
- **Handle Legal and Tax Matters**: Trusts have legal and tax implications, so the trustee will need to file tax returns for the trust, manage estate taxes, and deal with any legal issues that come up. They may need to hire attorneys, accountants, or financial advisors to help with this.
- **Communicate with Beneficiaries**: The trustee is also the point person for the beneficiaries, keeping them updated on the trust's status, answering questions, and managing any potential conflicts.

It's clear that being a trustee is more than just a title—it's a job. And not everyone is cut out for it. So how do you make sure you're picking the right person? Let's break it down.

QUALITIES OF A GOOD TRUSTEE

You'll want to choose someone who is **responsible, trustworthy**, and able to handle the legal and financial complexities that come with managing a trust. But let's get more specific—here are the key qualities to look for in a good trustee:

1. Trustworthiness

This seems obvious, but it's worth repeating: your trustee should be someone you **trust completely.** They'll be handling your hard- earned (or suddenly earned) money and making decisions that will impact your beneficiaries, so it's crucial that you choose someone with integrity. They need to follow your instructions to the letter, even if family members try to influence them otherwise.

2. Financial Savvy

Your trustee doesn't need to be Warren Buffet, but they should at least have a basic understanding of finances and investing. They'll be managing assets, handling distributions, and making decisions about investments, so financial literacy is a must. If they're completely clueless about money, they might end up making costly mistakes—or worse, they might fall for bad advice from others.

3. Organizational Skills

A trustee needs to be detail-oriented and organized. They'll have to keep track of the trust's assets, distributions, expenses, and taxes. If your trustee isn't the kind of person who can keep their own bills straight, they're probably not going to do a great job managing a trust. Look for someone who's responsible and capable of handling paperwork and deadlines.

4. Fairness and Impartiality

If you're planning to divide your trust among multiple beneficiaries (especially family members), it's essential that your trustee be **fair** and **impartial**. The trustee should be able to make decisions without playing favorites or getting caught up in family drama. This is especially important if your beneficiaries have competing interests or aren't on the best terms.

5. Willingness and Availability

Being a trustee is a long-term commitment, so your choice needs to be **willing** to take on the responsibility—and **available** to manage the trust over time. Some people just don't have the time or interest to handle the ongoing duties of a trustee, so make sure your trustee understands the job and is up for it. They should be available to act whenever the need arises, which can sometimes be unexpected.

WHO SHOULD YOU AVOID?

Now that you know what to look for in a trustee, let's talk about who you should **avoid** putting in charge of your trust:

1. Family Members with Conflicts of Interest

It might seem like a good idea to name a family member as trustee, but if that person is also a beneficiary, there's potential for **conflict of interest**. For example, if your trustee stands to inherit part of the trust, they might be tempted to make decisions that benefit themselves over other beneficiaries. If you do name a family member, make sure they're someone who can stay neutral and act in the best interest of everyone involved.

2. Someone Who's Easily Swayed

If your trustee is the kind of person who says "yes" to everything, they might not be the best choice. Trust management can involve tough decisions, and your trustee may need to say "no" to beneficiaries who ask for early payouts or more money than they're entitled to. You don't want someone who will cave under pressure or be guilted into making decisions that go against your wishes.

3. People with No Financial Experience

A trustee who doesn't understand basic financial principles could end up making bad decisions that hurt the trust's value. You might love your brother, but if he thinks "diversification" is a new kind of salad, he's probably not the best person to manage your trust.

Choose someone with at least some understanding of how money works—or someone who's willing to hire professionals for help.

4. Someone with a Lot on Their Plate

The job of a trustee can be time-consuming, so if your potential trustee is already overwhelmed with work, family obligations, or personal issues, they might not have the bandwidth to manage the trust effectively. Look for someone who has the time and capacity to take on the role without getting overwhelmed.

SHOULD YOU CHOOSE A PROFESSIONAL TRUSTEE?

If you're struggling to find someone in your circle who fits the bill, don't worry—you can always hire a **professional trustee.** Many banks, trust companies, and law firms offer trust management services. While professional trustees charge fees (usually a percentage of the trust's value), they bring expertise, experience, and impartiality to the table. Plus, they're less likely to get caught up in family drama.

Here's why you might want to go with a professional trustee:

- **Expertise**: A professional trustee will have experience managing trusts, dealing with legal and tax issues, and handling investments. They'll be able to navigate complex situations that an inexperienced trustee might struggle with.
- **Impartiality**: Professional trustees don't have personal connections to the beneficiaries, so they can remain neutral and make fair decisions without being influenced by emotions or family dynamics.
- **Longevity**: If your trust is designed to last for a long time (like a **dynasty trust**), a professional trustee ensures continuity. People retire, pass away, or become unavailable, but professional trustees can continue managing the trust for generations.

However, there are some downsides to professional trustees. They can be expensive, and they might not have the personal touch that a trusted family member or friend would bring. You'll also need to find a company or institution that you feel comfortable with.

CO-TRUSTEES: DOUBLE THE PROTECTION?

If you can't decide between a family member and a professional trustee, why not choose both? **Co-trustees** allow you to split the responsibilities. For example, you could name a trusted family member as a co-trustee alongside a professional. This gives you the best of both worlds: the personal involvement of someone you know and the expertise of a professional.

Here's how it could work:

- The family member handles day-to-day decisions and communications with the beneficiaries, while the professional trustee takes care of the financial management and legal issues.
- Both trustees have to agree on major decisions, which adds an extra layer of protection to ensure that your wishes are followed.

THE BOTTOM LINE

Choosing a trustee is one of the most critical decisions you'll make when setting up a trust. Whether you choose a trusted family member, a close friend, or a professional trustee, the person (or team) you select will have a huge impact on how well your trust is managed and how smoothly your wealth is passed on.

Remember, your trustee needs to be trustworthy, financially savvy, and able to handle the legal and logistical complexities that come with managing a trust. They'll be the one making sure your wishes are followed and that your wealth is protected for future generations.

In the next chapter, we'll explore the different kinds of trusts you can use to protect your assets while you're alive—starting with the **living trust** and why it's one of the most versatile tools in wealth management. Stay tuned!

MIKE MARKUSON

CHAPTER 7: LIVING THE DREAM: HOW TO USE A LIVING TRUST

Summary:

Want to keep control over your assets while you're alive but still protect them for the future? Enter the living trust! In this chapter, we'll explain what a living trust is, how it works, and why it's a great option for people who want to maintain control while preparing for the inevitable.

You might be wondering, "Why not just wait and let my will handle everything when I'm gone?" Well, a living trust offers some major advantages that a simple will just can't match. Here's why you should consider setting one up now:

1. Avoiding Probate

Probate is like the DMV of the legal world—long, complicated, and a real headache. When you pass away, your will has to go through probate, where a court validates it and oversees the distribution of your assets. This process can take months or even years, and it often comes with hefty fees that cut into your estate.

With a living trust, your assets skip the whole probate process. Since the trust technically owns your assets (and not you), they can be transferred to your beneficiaries immediately, privately, and without court involvement. No lawyers, no judges, no public records—it's quick, easy, and drama-free.

2. Maintaining Control While You're Alive

One of the best parts of a living trust is that you're still in charge. Unlike an irrevocable trust, where you give up control over your assets, a living trust allows you to manage your money and property just like before. Want to sell that vacation home? Go for it. Need to add new assets to the trust? No problem. You can change the terms of the trust or even dissolve it completely if your situation changes. You're in the driver's seat the whole time.

3. Planning for Incapacity

We don't like to think about it, but there's always the chance that you might become unable to manage your own affairs due to illness or injury. A living trust gives you a built-in backup plan. If something happens to you and you're no longer able to manage your assets, your **successor trustee** steps in to handle things on your behalf. They can take care of your finances, manage your property, and pay your bills—all without the need for a court-appointed guardian or conservator. It's like having a financial safety net for your future.

4. Privacy

Wills go through probate, which is a public process. That means anyone can look up how your estate was divided, who got what, and how much money was involved. If you value your privacy, a living trust is a much better option. Since trusts don't go through probate, everything stays confidential—no public records, no nosy neighbors, no unwanted attention.

5. Handling Out-of-State Property

If you own property in more than one state, things can get complicated fast when it comes to probate. Each state has its own probate laws, and your beneficiaries could end up dealing with multiple probate courts (and paying multiple sets of fees) to settle your estate. A living trust makes this easy. Since the trust owns your property, everything is handled in one place—no matter where your assets are located.

TYPES OF LIVING TRUSTS

Just like shoes, living trusts come in a variety of styles. Let's take a quick look at the two most common types and how they differ:

1. Revocable Living Trust

This is the most popular type of living trust because it's flexible and easy to set up. A **revocable living trust** allows you to make changes whenever you want—add or remove assets, change beneficiaries, or even dissolve the trust entirely. You're in full control, which is perfect if you like the idea of having options.

Since the trust is revocable, you can pull assets in and out as needed. However, the downside is that revocable trusts don't offer much protection from creditors, lawsuits, or taxes because the IRS and the courts still see the assets as yours. You're still responsible for paying taxes on income generated by the trust, and if someone sues you, your trust assets could be at risk.

2. Irrevocable Living Trust

On the other hand, an **irrevocable living trust** is more like a financial vault—once you put assets in, you can't easily take them out. This type of trust is much more restrictive because you give up control over the assets. However, the trade-off is that an irrevocable trust offers much better protection from creditors and lawsuits. Plus, the assets in the trust are no longer considered part of your estate, so they won't be hit with estate taxes when you pass away.

Irrevocable trusts are ideal for people who are more focused on asset protection and tax savings than flexibility. But remember: once it's set up, you can't easily make changes. It's a one-way street.

SETTING UP A LIVING TRUST: STEP-BY-STEP

If you're thinking a living trust might be right for you, here's a quick guide to getting started:

1. Make an Inventory of Your Assets

First, take stock of what you own. This includes real estate, bank accounts, investments, retirement accounts, life insurance policies, and personal property like cars, jewelry, and valuable collections. These are the assets you'll be transferring into the trust.

2. Choose a Trustee and Successor Trustee

As with any trust, you'll need to pick a **trustee** (which will likely be you, since you're managing the trust while you're alive). But more importantly, you'll need to choose a **successor trustee**—someone to take over when you're no longer able to manage the trust. This could be a trusted family member, friend, or a professional trustee, depending on your situation.

3. Create the Trust Document

You'll need to work with a lawyer to draft the trust document. This is the legal paperwork that spells out the terms of the trust, including who the beneficiaries are, how the assets should be managed, and when distributions will be made.

4. Transfer Ownership of Your Assets

Once the trust is set up, you'll need to transfer ownership of your assets into the trust. This means changing the title of your property, bank accounts, and other assets so that the trust is now the legal owner. Don't worry, you still get to control everything—you're just putting it under the trust's name for legal purposes.

5. Review and Update the Trust as Needed

Your living trust is flexible, so make sure you review it regularly and update it as your situation changes. If you buy new property, have more kids, or decide to change beneficiaries, it's easy to make adjustments.

THE BOTTOM LINE

A **living trust** is one of the most versatile and powerful tools you can use to manage your wealth while you're alive and plan for a smooth transfer of assets after you're gone. It gives you the flexibility to stay in control of your assets, avoid probate, and plan for incapacity—all while keeping things private and easy for your loved ones.

Whether you go with a revocable or irrevocable living trust, the key is to set one up while you're still in good health and able to make decisions. It's a proactive way to protect your wealth, take care of your family, and ensure that your wishes are followed without the hassle of probate or court intervention.

In the next chapter, we'll talk about one of the most misunderstood topics in trust planning: **trust funds.** You don't have to be a billionaire to set one up, and they're not just for spoiled rich kids. Trust funds are a great way to ensure your money is used the way you want—even after you're gone. Stay tuned!

CHAPTER 8: TRUST FUNDS AREN'T JUST FOR THE SUPER RICH

Summary:

Forget the stereotype of spoiled trust fund kids. In this chapter, we'll explain how setting up a trust fund can benefit anyone, especially if you've just come into sudden wealth. Whether it's for your kids, grandkids, or a good cause, you'll learn how a trust fund can make sure your money goes exactly where you want it to.

When most people hear the words **"trust fund,"** they immediately picture a mansion-dwelling, polo-playing, spoiled rich kid living off a pile of money they never earned. While it's true that many wealthy families use trust funds to secure their fortunes for future generations, you don't need to be a billionaire to benefit from one.

In fact, trust funds can be an incredibly useful tool for **anyone** who wants to make sure their money is used the way they intend— whether it's for their kids, grandkids, or even a charity.

In this chapter, we'll break down what a trust fund is (hint: it's not just for the 1%), why you might want to set one up, and how it can ensure that your wealth is managed responsibly long after you're gone. Spoiler: it's about way more than just handing

MIKE MARKUSON

over piles of cash.

WHAT EXACTLY IS A TRUST FUND?

At its core, a **trust fund** is simply money or other assets that have been set aside in a trust to benefit someone else. The **trustee** manages the assets according to the terms you set when you create the trust, and the **beneficiaries** (your kids, grandkids, or whomever you choose) receive those benefits in the way you specify.

But here's the kicker: trust funds are incredibly **flexible.** You're in total control of when and how the money is distributed. You can give your beneficiaries a one-time payout, provide regular payments, or set up specific conditions that must be met before they get anything. Want to make sure your kids finish college before they touch the money? You can do that. Want to ensure your money is used responsibly and not blown on sports cars? You can do that too.

Essentially, a trust fund gives you control beyond the grave, ensuring your money goes where you want, when you want, and for the reasons you want.

WHO CAN BENEFIT FROM A TRUST FUND?

Contrary to popular belief, you don't need a **massive** fortune to set up a trust fund. In fact, it can be a great financial tool for **anyone** with assets they want to protect and pass down responsibly. Here's who can benefit from a trust fund:

1. Parents with Young Kids

If you've got young children, a trust fund can be one of the smartest ways to ensure they're taken care of if something happens to you.

You can set up the trust so your kids receive financial support when they need it, but you control how and when the money is distributed. This way, they won't inherit a massive sum at 18 and go wild with it.

You can set conditions like:

- Receiving money only for education-related expenses.
- Distributing funds in stages—maybe a portion at 25, another at 30, and so on.
- Using the trust to pay for specific needs like housing or medical care, rather than giving them free rein.

2. Adults with Special Needs

If you have a family member with special needs, a **special needs trust** ensures that they're financially supported without affecting their eligibility for government assistance programs like Medicaid or Social Security. The trust fund provides for their care and expenses while protecting their ability to receive benefits.

3. People Who Want to Avoid Family Conflict

Worried about potential **family drama** over your assets when you're gone? A trust fund helps you avoid the "who gets what" fights by laying down specific rules for how your money is distributed. This ensures that everyone knows your exact wishes and can't argue over the division of your estate.

4. Charitable Givers

Want to leave part of your estate to a favorite charity? A **charitable trust fund** can be set up to donate money over time or in a lump sum. You can even set it up to benefit your family first and then pass the remaining assets to charity after a certain period or after your beneficiaries have passed on.

5. Entrepreneurs and Business Owners

If you own a family business or significant assets, a trust fund can help ensure that those assets are passed down in a way that aligns with your long-term goals. You can provide instructions for how your business should be managed or sold and distribute the proceeds to your family in a structured way.

TYPES OF TRUST FUNDS

There's no one-size-fits-all when it comes to trust funds, which is why they're so powerful. You can create a trust fund that's tailored to your specific goals. Here are a few of the most common types of trust funds and what they're best suited for:

1. Revocable Trust Fund

A **revocable trust fund** allows you to stay in control of the assets during your lifetime, and you can make changes to the trust whenever you want. This is a great option if you're not quite sure how you want to distribute your money yet, or if your financial situation is likely to change. The downside is that since you retain control of the assets, they are still considered part of your estate for tax purposes.

2. Irrevocable Trust Fund

An **irrevocable trust fund** is more permanent—once it's set up, you can't easily change or revoke it. However, the assets in the trust are no longer considered part of your estate, which means they're protected from estate taxes and creditors. This type of trust fund is ideal if you're focused on long-term estate planning, asset protection, and reducing taxes.

3. Spendthrift Trust

Worried that your beneficiaries might blow through their inheritance like it's Monopoly money? A **spendthrift trust** is designed to protect assets from reckless spending. The trustee controls the distributions, and the beneficiary can only access the money under certain conditions. This is a great option if you want to prevent a beneficiary from wasting their inheritance or getting into financial trouble.

4. Special Needs Trust

A **special needs trust** ensures that a beneficiary with a disability receives financial support without jeopardizing their eligibility for government benefits. The trustee manages the funds, and the money is used to pay for medical expenses, housing, education, and other needs not covered by government programs.

5. Charitable Trust

A **charitable trust** is a fantastic way to give back while also enjoying some tax benefits. You can set up a charitable trust to donate assets to a favorite charity while still providing for your family. One popular option is a **charitable remainder trust**, which provides income to your beneficiaries for a period of time, with the remainder going to charity.

HOW TO STRUCTURE YOUR TRUST FUND

One of the most powerful features of a trust fund is that you get to decide exactly **how** the money is managed and distributed. Here are a few options for structuring your trust fund to fit your specific goals:

1. Staggered Distributions

If you're worried about handing over a large sum of money all at once, you can set up the trust to distribute funds in stages. For example, your kids might get 25% of the trust when they turn 25, another 25% at 30, and the rest at 35. This gives them time to mature and learn to manage their money responsibly.

2. Conditional Distributions

Want to make sure your beneficiaries meet certain criteria before they get their inheritance? You can set conditions like requiring them to finish college, hold down a steady job, or stay free of legal trouble before they can access the funds. This is a great way to encourage good behavior while still providing financial support.

3. Discretionary Trust

A **discretionary trust** gives the trustee full control over when and how the money is distributed. The trustee decides how much money the beneficiaries receive based on their needs. This can be useful if you're unsure how much support your beneficiaries will need or if you trust the trustee to make responsible decisions on your behalf.

4. Education-Specific Trust

If your primary goal is to fund your kids' or grandkids' education, you can set up the trust to pay for tuition, books, and other
education-related expenses. This ensures that your money is used for its intended purpose and that your beneficiaries get the financial support they need to succeed.

COMMON MYTHS ABOUT TRUST FUNDS

Let's clear up a few misconceptions about trust funds that might be holding you back from setting one up:

Myth 1: Trust Funds Are Only for the Ultra-Wealthy

False! While the ultra-wealthy do use trust funds, they're not exclusive to the super-rich. If you have assets you want to protect, even a modest amount, a trust fund can be a smart tool for ensuring those assets are managed and distributed according to your wishes.

Myth 2: Trust Funds Spoil Kids

Trust funds get a bad rap thanks to stories of trust-fund babies living lavish, irresponsible lifestyles. But in reality, a well-structured trust fund can do the opposite—it can teach responsibility and ensure that your money is used wisely. By setting conditions and structuring distributions, you can encourage your beneficiaries to make smart decisions.

Myth 3: Trust Funds Are Complicated and Expensive to Set Up

Setting up a trust fund does require legal help, but it doesn't have to be overly complicated or expensive. With the help of a good estate planning attorney, you can set up a trust fund that fits your needs without breaking the bank.

THE BOTTOM LINE

Trust funds aren't just for the super-rich or the elite. They're a smart, flexible tool for **anyone** who wants to ensure their money is managed responsibly and used in line with their wishes. Whether you're looking to take care of your kids, protect a loved one with special needs, or leave a legacy to charity, a trust fund gives you total control over how your wealth is distributed.

The best part? You get to set the rules. You can prevent reckless spending, reward good behavior, and make sure your beneficiaries get the financial support they need—without putting them in a position to fail.

In the next chapter, we'll tackle the importance of **protecting your assets**—not just from others, but from yourself. Stay tuned for some practical tips on how to shield your wealth from creditors, lawsuits, and even your own bad spending habits!

TRUST ISSUES: A BEGINNER'S GUIDE TO PROTECTING YOUR NEW FORTUNE

CHAPTER 9: PROTECTING YOUR ASSETS FROM EVERYONE, INCLUDING YOURSELF

Summary:

When the money rolls in, so do the opportunists. This chapter is all about using trusts to protect your assets from lawsuits, creditors, and even your own bad spending habits. Learn how to shield your wealth so that you can live comfortably without worrying about losing it all to a lawsuit or impulsive spending spree.

So, you've come into sudden wealth—congratulations! Whether it's from a lottery win, a smart investment, or the much-anticipated revaluation of foreign currency, the financial freedom you've dreamed about is finally here. But with that freedom comes responsibility, and one of the most important responsibilities is making sure your new fortune stays safe. The reality is that as much as we love the idea of being rich, wealth can attract all kinds of problems—from creditors and lawsuits to, well, your own impulsive spending habits.

In this chapter, we're going to look at how you can **protect your assets**, not just from outside threats, but also from the temptations that can come with sudden wealth. Trusts are a powerful tool in this defense strategy, but there are some other techniques you should know about to make sure your money stays where it belongs— secure, protected, and under your control.

WHY YOU NEED ASSET PROTECTION

Wealth can change your life for the better, but it also puts a target on your back. Once people know you've come into money, creditors, opportunists, and even family members might come looking for a piece of the pie. Here's why **asset protection** should be a top priority for you:

1. Lawsuits

Sudden wealth makes you more vulnerable to lawsuits, whether from business disputes, personal injury claims, or even disgruntled acquaintances looking to cash in on your success. Without the right protections in place, you could lose a significant chunk of your assets to legal fees or settlements.

2. Creditors

If you've got outstanding debts or business liabilities, creditors might see your new wealth as a way to settle old scores. They can come after your assets to pay off debts, which could quickly reduce your fortune.

3. Divorce

Let's face it—divorce can be financially devastating, especially if you don't have a solid plan in place to protect your assets. Whether it's an unexpected split or a marriage you thought was rock solid, failing to plan for the worst can leave you with much less than you bargained for.

4. Reckless Spending

One of the biggest threats to sudden wealth isn't from outsiders —it's from you. Impulse buys, bad investments, or overly generous loans to family and friends can deplete your fortune faster than you'd think. That's why having some guardrails in place to protect yourself from yourself is so important.

HOW TRUSTS PROTECT YOUR WEALTH

As we've talked about in earlier chapters, **trusts** are one of the best ways to protect your assets. But how do they actually work when it comes to shielding your wealth from creditors, lawsuits, and even bad spending decisions? Let's break it down:

1. Irrevocable Trusts: Shielding Assets from Lawsuits and Creditors

If asset protection is your top priority, an **irrevocable trust** is one of the best tools you can use. Once you place your assets in an irrevocable trust, they are no longer considered part of your personal estate. This means that creditors and lawsuit claimants can't go after the assets in the trust because, legally, you don't own them anymore —the trust does.

An irrevocable trust is also a great way to protect your wealth in the event of divorce. Since the assets in the trust aren't part of your estate, they typically won't be included in divorce settlements.

However, keep in mind that once you set up an irrevocable trust, you give up control of the assets. This is why it's important to choose a trustworthy trustee and be sure you're ready to let go of direct ownership.

2. Spendthrift Trusts: Guarding Against Bad Decisions

A **spendthrift trust** is a great way to protect your beneficiaries — and yourself—from blowing through money too quickly. With a spendthrift trust, the trustee has full control over how and when money is distributed, preventing the beneficiaries from withdrawing large sums at once. This can be incredibly helpful if you're worried about irresponsible spending, either on your part or on the part of the people you're leaving money to.

For example, you can set up a trust that only allows a certain amount of money to be withdrawn each year, or that requires the trustee to approve larger expenses. This keeps your wealth from disappearing on a shopping spree or poorly thought-out investment.

3. Asset Protection Trusts: A Stronger Defense

An **asset protection trust** (APT) is specifically designed to shield your wealth from creditors and lawsuits. These trusts are typically set up offshore (in places like the Cook Islands or Nevis) to provide maximum protection. With an APT, it's extremely difficult for creditors or legal claimants to access the trust's assets, making it one of the most robust forms of asset protection available.

However, offshore trusts can be expensive to set up and maintain, and they come with a higher level of scrutiny. But if you're looking to go the extra mile in protecting your assets, this type of trust might be worth considering.

OTHER ASSET PROTECTION STRATEGIES

While trusts are one of the best ways to protect your wealth, there are other strategies you can use to add even more layers of security. Here are some additional steps you can take to safeguard your fortune:

1. Limited Liability Companies (LLCs)

If you own property, run a business, or hold valuable assets, consider setting up a **Limited Liability Company (LLC)** to hold those assets. By placing property or investments into an LLC, you create a legal barrier between those assets and your personal wealth. This way, if someone sues you personally, they can't go after the assets held in the LLC.

Similarly, if you run a business, forming an LLC can protect your personal assets from business liabilities. If the business gets sued, only the assets owned by the business are at risk, not your personal fortune.

2. Insurance

You can never underestimate the importance of having the right **insurance** coverage. Liability insurance, umbrella insurance, and professional indemnity insurance can provide an additional safety net to protect your assets in case of lawsuits or unexpected events. The goal is to make sure that if something goes wrong, the insurance company pays the bills—not you.

3. Prenuptial Agreements

If you're married or planning to get married, a **prenuptial agreement** is an important part of asset protection. While it might not be the most romantic topic, a prenup helps ensure that your assets stay protected in case of divorce. Without one, your spouse could have legal rights to a large portion of your wealth, which could significantly reduce your estate.

4. Debt Management

Managing and reducing your debt is another form of asset protection. The less you owe, the less vulnerable you are to creditors coming after your wealth. If you've suddenly come into money, it might be tempting to ignore your debts or let them slide, but paying off high-interest debts early can save you a fortune in the long run and reduce the risk of future financial problems.

Protecting Yourself from Impulsive Spending

One of the biggest threats to your wealth isn't from creditors or lawsuits—it's from **impulse spending**. It's easy to splurge when you suddenly have a lot of money, but if you're not careful, it can disappear faster than you'd expect. Here's how you can protect your assets from your own impulses:

1. Set Up a Budget

It might sound basic, but creating a budget is one of the best ways to stay on track financially. Set limits for how much you'll spend on big-ticket items, and stick to those limits. You can still enjoy your newfound wealth, but having a budget in place will keep you from blowing it all on things you don't really need.

2. Use a Trustee for Major Decisions

If you're setting up a trust for yourself, consider appointing a **co-trustee** or someone else who has to approve large withdrawals. This adds a layer of accountability and can help you think twice before making major purchases or risky investments.

3. Automate Savings

Set up automatic transfers to savings accounts or investment portfolios to make sure you're consistently setting money aside for the future. This way, even if you're tempted to spend, a portion of your wealth is automatically being protected.

THE BOTTOM LINE

When you come into sudden wealth, protecting that fortune is just as important as growing it. Whether it's from lawsuits, creditors, or your own impulses, there are plenty of threats that can drain your bank account if you're not careful. But with the right strategies in place—like setting up irrevocable trusts, LLCs, and spendthrift clauses—you can safeguard your assets and ensure your money stays secure for the long haul.

Trusts aren't just for the ultra-wealthy or for managing inheritances
—they're a powerful tool for protecting wealth in all its forms, especially when you've suddenly come into money. So, take the time to set up your financial defenses, and you'll thank yourself later when your fortune stays safe, sound, and under your control.

In the next and final chapter, we'll dive into **how to set up a trust without losing your mind**—a practical step-by-step guide to getting all of this in motion so you can start protecting your wealth today!

TRUST ISSUES: A BEGINNER'S GUIDE TO PROTECTING YOUR NEW FORTUNE

CHAPTER 10: THE FINAL STEP: HOW TO SET UP A TRUST (WITHOUT LOSING YOUR MIND)

Summary:

Ready to get started? We'll wrap things up with a step- by-step guide to setting up a trust. From picking the right lawyer to gathering the necessary documents, this chapter will guide you through the process in plain English, so you can protect your new fortune without breaking a sweat. We'll also include some common mistakes to avoid and a checklist to keep you on track.

You've made it this far! You now know the ins and outs of trusts, how they protect your wealth, and why they're one of the best tools for managing your newfound fortune. But now comes the real question: **How do you actually set one up?** Don't worry—it's not as complicated as it sounds. By the end of this chapter, you'll have a clear, step-by-step guide to setting up a trust, so you can start protecting your assets and securing your financial future.

Let's take the mystery out of the process and break it down into easy, manageable steps. Trust me—pun intended—it'll be worth it.

STEP 1: DEFINE YOUR GOALS

Before you can set up a trust, you need to ask yourself: **What are you trying to accomplish?** The kind of trust you create, and how you structure it, will depend on what you want to achieve.

Here are some questions to help define your goals:
- **Who do you want to benefit?** (Kids, grandkids, charities, etc.)
- **When should they receive the money?** (All at once, at certain ages, or over time?)
- **Do you want to retain control or give up control?** (Revocable vs. irrevocable trust)
- **Are you trying to reduce taxes, protect assets, or both?**
- **Do you want to protect beneficiaries from bad spending habits?** (Consider a spendthrift trust)
- **Do you want to plan for special situations, like caring for someone with special needs?**

Take some time to think about your goals. The clearer you are about what you want to accomplish, the easier the process will be—and the better the outcome.

Step 2: Choose the Type of Trust

Once you know your goals, it's time to decide on the **type of trust** that best suits your needs. We've covered the various types in previous chapters, but here's a quick recap:
- **Revocable Trust**: Gives you control while you're alive and can be changed at any time. Great for flexibility but

offers less protection from creditors and taxes.

- **Irrevocable Trust**: Once set up, it can't be easily changed, but it offers strong protection from creditors, lawsuits, and estate taxes.
- **Spendthrift Trust**: Protects beneficiaries from blowing their inheritance by giving the trustee control over how and when the money is distributed.
- **Special Needs Trust**: Ensures that someone with special needs is cared for without affecting their eligibility for government benefits.
- **Charitable Trust**: Allows you to leave part of your wealth to a charity while still benefiting your family or receiving an income stream.
- **Asset Protection Trust**: Provides the highest level of protection from creditors and lawsuits, often set up offshore.

Choosing the right trust is essential for achieving your goals, so make sure you pick the one that aligns with your priorities.

STEP 3: PICK A TRUSTEE

As we covered in Chapter 6, choosing the right **trustee** is a crucial step in setting up your trust. This person (or institution) will be responsible for managing the trust, making decisions, and distributing the assets according to your wishes. Here's a quick refresher on what to consider:

- **Trustworthiness**: The trustee should be someone who will follow your instructions to the letter.
- **Financial Know-How**: They need to understand the financial and legal aspects of managing a trust.
- **Impartiality**: They should be able to act fairly and without bias, especially if there are multiple beneficiaries.
- **Availability**: Make sure they have the time and willingness to take on the responsibility.

You can also hire a **professional trustee**—like a bank or trust company—if you don't have someone in your personal life who fits the bill. If you're unsure, consider appointing **co-trustees**, which gives you the benefit of having both a trusted family member and a professional managing the trust together.

STEP 4: CREATE THE TRUST DOCUMENT

Now it's time to **get legal.** You'll need to work with an estate planning attorney to draft the trust document, which is the legal paperwork that sets up the trust and spells out the rules for how it operates. Here's what the trust document will include:

- **The Name of the Trust**: This can be something simple like "The [Your Name] Family Trust."
- **The Trustee**: This is the person or institution you're appointing to manage the trust.
- **The Beneficiaries**: The people or organizations who will benefit from the trust.
- **The Terms of the Trust**: This is where you outline the rules
  —when the beneficiaries will receive the money, any conditions they need to meet, and how the trustee should manage the assets.
- **The Assets**: A list of the assets you're transferring into the trust, such as real estate, bank accounts, stocks, or personal property.
- **The Successor Trustee**: This is the person who will take over if the original trustee is unable to continue managing the trust.

An experienced attorney will help you navigate this process and ensure that everything is legally sound and aligned with your wishes. While there are online tools that let you create a trust yourself, it's best to work with a professional for something as important as your financial legacy.

STEP 5: FUND THE TRUST

Creating the trust document is just the beginning. Once it's set up, you need to **fund the trust** by transferring ownership of your assets into it. This is the step where many people get tripped up, so let's go over it in detail.

What Does It Mean to "Fund" the Trust?

Funding the trust simply means transferring assets from your name into the name of the trust. For example, if you own a house, you would change the title so that the trust is the legal owner. If you have bank accounts or investments, you would transfer those accounts into the trust's name.

How to Transfer Different Types of Assets:

- **Real Estate**: You'll need to update the property title with your local government to reflect the trust as the new owner.

- **Bank Accounts and Investments**: Contact your bank or financial institution and request that your accounts be transferred into the trust's name. This usually requires some paperwork but is a straightforward process.

- **Life Insurance and Retirement Accounts**: You can't transfer these directly into a trust, but you can name the trust as the beneficiary. This ensures that the payout goes to the trust when you pass away, rather than going

through probate.
- **Personal Property**: For high-value items like cars, art, or jewelry, you can transfer ownership to the trust through a bill of sale or another legal document.

It's important to work with your attorney or financial advisor during this process to make sure everything is transferred correctly. If you forget to fund the trust, the assets won't be protected by it!

STEP 6: REVIEW AND UPDATE THE TRUST

Setting up a trust is not a "set it and forget it" task. As your life changes, you'll need to **review and update** your trust to reflect those changes. Here are some common reasons to update your trust:

- **New Assets**: If you acquire new property, investments, or other assets, make sure to add them to the trust.
- **Changes in Beneficiaries**: Life happens—people get married, have children, or pass away. Make sure your trust reflects your current relationships and intentions.
- **Legal Changes**: Tax laws and estate planning rules change over time. It's a good idea to review your trust with an attorney every few years to make sure it's still the best strategy for your financial situation.
- **Health Changes**: If your health declines or you foresee needing long-term care, you may want to make adjustments to your trust to account for medical expenses or to ensure that your wealth is protected.

Regularly reviewing your trust ensures that it continues to meet your goals and that no important assets are left out.

STEP 7: COMMUNICATE WITH YOUR FAMILY

One of the most overlooked parts of setting up a trust is **communicating with your beneficiaries** about your plans. While you don't need to share all the details, it's important to let your family know that you've set up a trust and explain the general guidelines for how it works. This can help avoid confusion, misunderstandings, and even family conflict after you're gone.

You should also introduce your beneficiaries to your trustee (or successor trustee) and explain why you've chosen them for the job.

Open communication helps ensure that your wishes are followed smoothly and reduces the risk of family disputes.

THE BOTTOM LINE

Setting up a trust is one of the best things you can do to protect your wealth and ensure that it's passed on according to your wishes.

While the process might seem daunting at first, it's actually quite manageable if you break it down into steps. By defining your goals, choosing the right trust, picking a trustworthy trustee, and funding the trust properly, you'll be well on your way to securing your financial legacy.

Remember, trusts aren't just for the ultra-wealthy—they're for anyone who wants to protect their assets, avoid probate, reduce taxes, and ensure their money is used responsibly. Whether you're dealing with a sudden windfall or simply planning for the future, a trust gives you control, security, and peace of mind.

Now that you've reached the final chapter, you've got all the tools you need to take action and make smart decisions about your wealth. So, what are you waiting for? It's time to take that first step toward **protecting your fortune** for yourself and the people you care about most.

CHAPTER 11: IN CONCLUSION

Summary:

The final chapter recaps the key lessons from the eBook and emphasizes the importance of consulting a lawyer or trust professional to tailor your trust plan to your unique situation. It reminds readers that trust planning is an ongoing process that requires expert guidance to ensure long-term success.

You've made it to the finish line! Over the past chapters, we've covered the essential aspects of trusts and asset protection, demystifying a topic that can seem complicated at first. Whether you're anticipating sudden wealth, already rolling in it, or just planning ahead, you now have a solid understanding of how trusts can help you protect your fortune, manage your assets, and keep your money working for you and your loved ones.

But here's the thing: while this eBook has given you a strong **introduction** to the world of trusts, it's important to recognize that every individual's situation is different, and the rules around trusts can be complex. That's why it's absolutely essential to **consult with a lawyer or trust professional** before making any big decisions.

In this final chapter, we'll recap the key takeaways and remind you why professional advice is crucial as you move forward with your wealth protection plans.

WHAT YOU'VE LEARNED SO FAR

We've covered a lot of ground in this eBook. Here's a quick refresher of the most important points:

1. Trusts Are Powerful Tools for Wealth Protection

Trusts can help you avoid probate, minimize taxes, protect your assets from creditors, and ensure your wealth is distributed according to your wishes. They are flexible, customizable, and can be tailored to fit your unique financial situation.

2. There's a Trust for Every Situation

Whether you're setting up a **revocable trust** to maintain control, an **irrevocable trust** for tax and lawsuit protection, a **spendthrift trust** to protect beneficiaries from overspending, or a **special needs trust** to care for a loved one, there's a trust that's right for you.

3. Choosing the Right Trustee is Crucial

Your trustee is the person who will carry out your wishes and manage your trust. They need to be trustworthy, financially savvy, and capable of handling the responsibilities that come with managing your assets.

4. Trusts Protect You from More Than Just Creditors

In addition to safeguarding your wealth from lawsuits and creditors, trusts can protect you from your own bad spending habits or family disputes, ensuring that your money is used responsibly by those who inherit it.

5. Asset Protection Is a Long-Term Game

Setting up a trust is only the first step. You'll need to regularly review and update your trust to ensure it still aligns with your goals, reflects changes in your life, and complies with any new legal or tax regulations.

WHY YOU NEED PROFESSIONAL ADVICE

While this eBook has provided a **basic introduction** to trusts and wealth protection, it's important to remember that every financial situation is unique. Trust law is complicated, and there are many nuances and exceptions that could apply to your specific circumstances. That's why working with an experienced lawyer or trust professional is essential.

Here's why you shouldn't go it alone:

1. Tailoring the Trust to Your Needs

Your goals and assets are unique, and a trust needs to be customized to fit your particular situation. An estate planning attorney can help you design a trust that accomplishes exactly what you want— whether it's protecting your wealth, minimizing taxes, or ensuring the financial well-being of your family.

2. Avoiding Legal Pitfalls

Each state (and country) has different laws governing trusts and estate planning. Without professional guidance, you could run into legal issues, create a trust that doesn't accomplish your goals, or expose your assets to unnecessary risk. An attorney ensures that your trust is legally sound and compliant with the relevant laws.

3. Maximizing Tax Benefits

Trusts can offer significant tax benefits, but the rules are complex. A tax professional or attorney can help you take full advantage of the available tax strategies, ensuring that your trust minimizes taxes on your estate while maximizing the financial benefit to your heirs.

4. Keeping Things Up-to-Date

Trusts aren't "set it and forget it" tools—they need to be reviewed and updated regularly. Working with a professional ensures that your trust evolves as your life changes, whether that means adding new assets, changing beneficiaries, or adjusting the terms to reflect new goals.

THE BOTTOM LINE

Setting up a trust is one of the most important steps you can take to protect your wealth, provide for your loved ones, and make sure your financial legacy is secure. But even the most basic trust can involve complicated decisions and legal details that are easy to overlook. While this eBook has provided a helpful starting point, it's essential to work with a lawyer or estate planning professional to ensure that everything is done right.

So, take the information you've learned here, consult with a trusted advisor, and start building a plan that will protect your wealth for generations to come. By taking the time to get professional guidance, you'll ensure that your assets are safe, your family is cared for, and your hard-earned fortune is preserved.

Resources and Recommended Tools

Before you dive into the treasure trove of resources below, I want to be transparent with you. Some of the links I've included might be affiliate links, which means that if you decide to use them, I might earn a small commission—just a little extra to keep the lights on.

However, not all links are affiliate, and regardless of that, I only recommend tools and resources that I genuinely believe in and have found valuable in my own experience with trusts. These resources are designed to assist you on your journey, and I hope you find them as useful as I have!

The Nerd Picker Blog

http://nerdpicker.com

Proven Amazon Course

The Very Best Amazon Training Course!

http://provenamazoncourse.biz

My Facebook Biz page

http://www.facebook.com/TheNerdpicker

My Facebook Profile Page

http://facebook.com/michael.markuson

Silent Sales Machine Radio Podcast

http://bit.ly/SilentJim-Podcast

Free Facebook group for Amazon and Reselling (MST)

Pretty amazing group of over 75K members! https://bit.ly/MST-facebookgroup

I have 2 Youtube Channels – Please Subscribe to both (thanks)

https://www.youtube.com/@MichaelMarkusonTheNerdpicker and https://www.youtube.com/c/MichaelMarkuson

Backup your Data! Important!

https://bit.ly/backitupbiz

My Final Recommendation!

It is pretty amazing. Check it out on the next page...
Thanks

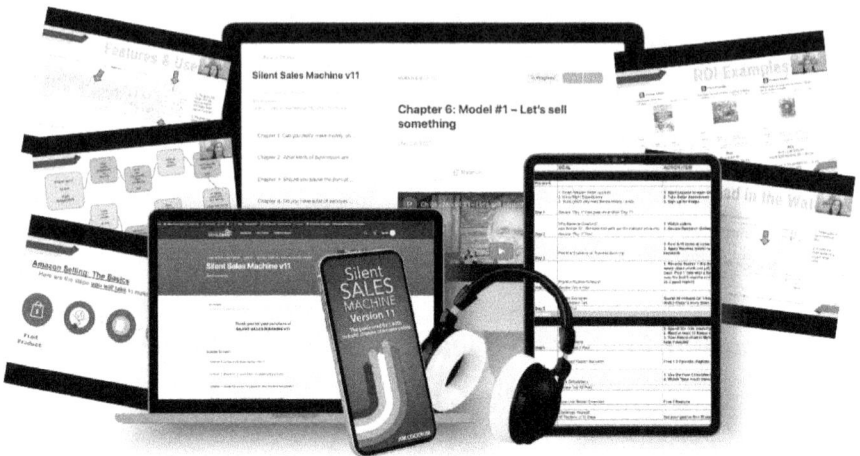

The complete step by step guide to create an 'Amazon Replens' business for $17.00 (95% off)

https://ko296.isrefer.com/go/ssmb/MMarkuson/

Here is what's included:

1. #1 Best Selling Book 'Silent Sales Machine', endorsed by Dave Ramsey, and read by over 1 million globally ($19 value).

2. The Amazon 101 Course with every detail needed (with step-by- step instructions) to get your first sale on Amazon ($297 value).

3. The Fast Start Guide that breaks down every step into an actionable 30 day plan to get to your first sale as fast as possible ($47 value).

You'll also get to interact with hundreds of students in our private Facebook group who replaced their 9-5 using this exact strategy. (Total value: $363).

Individually, we sell these items everyday in our store at this amount.

But our goal is to continue to be the largest community of Amazon sellers in the world, and collect even more success stories.

TRUST ISSUES: A BEGINNER'S GUIDE TO PROTECTING YOUR NEW FORTUNE

So Jim and his team and I decided to offer this bundle for only $17.00 (95% off), at this link:
https://ko296.isrefer.com/go/ssmb/MMarkuson/

Students using this method tell Jim's team all the time... Their biggest regret was waiting.

"Clocking in" everyday at a job they hated.

Almost letting fear stop them from walking away from their dead- end job forever.

But because of the Replens testing methods we teach, they realized there was nothing to be afraid of to begin with.

Click the link below to discover the exact, proven step-by-step process we use to replace our 9-5 job and build a life of freedom and abundance:

https://ko296.isrefer.com/go/ssmb/MMarkuson/

As you explore Amazon Replens on the next page, I hope it stirs something powerful in you about what is possible.

Thanks and God Bless..

Mike

www.ingramcontent.com/pod-product-compliance
Lightning Source LLC
Chambersburg PA
CBHW050312230526
45471CB00005B/2148